DREAM every day.

We know what we
are, but know not
what we may be.

WILLIAM SHAKESPEARE

DREAM every day.

We don't have
an eternity to
realize our
dreams, only the
time we are here.

SUSAN KING TAYLOR

Follow your dreams.
They know the way.

KOBI YAMADA

DREAM every day.

The human race
does command its
own destiny and
that destiny can
eventually embrace
the stars.

LORRAINE HANSBERRY

DREAM every day.

In life, there
are no ordinary
moments. Most
of us never really
recognize the
most significant
moments of our
lives when they're
happening.

KATHLEEN MAGEE

DREAM every day.

The greatest waste
in the world is the
difference between
what we are and
what we could
become.

BEN HERBSTER

DREAM every day.

When you reach
the top, that's
when the climb
begins.

MICHAEL CAINE

DREAM every day.

If you don't
have a dream,
how are you going
to have a dream
come true?

FAYE LAPOINTE

DREAM every day.

It is by tiny steps
that we ascend to
the stars.

JACK LEEDSTROM

DREAM every day.

Ah, but a man's
reach should
exceed his grasp,
or what's a
heaven for?

ROBERT BROWNING

DREAM every day.

Reminding one
another of the
dream that each
of us aspires to
may be enough
for us to set each
other free.

ANTOINE DE SAINT-EXUPERY

DREAM every day.

Some of the
world's greatest
feats were accom-
plished by people
not smart enough
to know they
were impossible.

DOUG LARSON

DREAM every day.

I've failed over
and over and over
again in my life.
And that is why
I succeed.

MICHAEL JORDAN

DREAM every day.

Life is a series of
collisions with the
future; it is not the
sum of what we
have been, but
what we yearn to be.

JOSE ORTEGA Y GASSET

DREAM every day.

Destiny is not a
thing to be waited
for, it is a thing
to be achieved.

WILLIAM JENNINGS BRYAN

DREAM every day.

To accomplish
great things, we
must not only plan,
but also believe.

ANATOLE FRANCE

DREAM every day.

I seldom think about
my limitations, and
they never make
me sad. Perhaps
there is just a touch
of yearning at times;
but it is vague,
like a breeze among
flowers.

HELEN KELLER

DREAM every day.

I love those
who yearn for
the impossible.

JOHANN VON GOETHE

DREAM every day.

No bird soars
too high if he
soars with his
own wings.

WILLIAM BLAKE

DREAM every day.

What do you pack
to pursue a dream,
and what do you
leave behind?

SANDRA SHARPE

DREAM every day.

To make a great
dream come true,
you must first have
a great dream.

HANS SELYE

DREAM every day.

Dreams take long-term commitments. From the first to the last, we need focus, discipline, persistence, and the ability to keep sight of the vision of what we are slowly creating.

DENNIS WHOLEY

DREAM every day.

Your dreams are
alive. They live
through you. Take
good care of them.

KOBI YAMADA

DREAM every day.

If you know what
you want, you
will recognize it
when you see it.

BILL COSBY

DREAM every day.

What you focus
on increases.

ROB ESTES

DREAM every day.

If you are on a
road to nowhere,
find another road.

ASHANTI PROVERB

DREAM every day.

Things may come
to those who wait,
but only the
things left by
those who hustle.

ABRAHAM LINCOLN

DREAM every day.

The aim, if
reached or not,
makes great
the life.

ROBERT BROWNING

DREAM every day.

We have enough people who tell it like it is—now we could use a few who tell it like it can be.

ROBERT ORBEN

DREAM every day.

Always keep one still,
secret spot where
dreams may go and,
sheltered so,
may thrive and grow.

LOUISE PRISCOLL

DREAM every day.

Just remember
that you don't
have to be what
they want you
to be.

MUHAMMAD ALI

DREAM every day.

Wide awake,
I can make my
most fantastic
dreams come true.

LORENTZ HART

DREAM every day.

No one has ever
seen tomorrow.

STEVEN FORTERE

DREAM every day.

People will try to
tell you that all the
great opportunities
have been snapped
up. In reality,
the world changes
every second,
blowing new
opportunities in
all directions,
including yours.

KEN HAKUTA

DREAM every day.

Often you just
have to rely on
your intuition.

BILL GATES

DREAM every day.

Sometimes you
just have to take
the leap, and
build your wings
on the way down.

KOBI YAMADA

DREAM every day.

The vision that
you glorify in
your mind,
the ideal that you
enthrone in your
heart—this you
will build your
life by, this you
will become.

JAMES ALLEN

DREAM every day.

If we did all
the things we
are capable of,
we would literally
astound ourselves.

THOMAS EDISON

DREAM every day.

If one advances
confidently in
the direction of
his dreams, and
endeavors to live
the life which he
has imagined, he
will meet with a
success unexpected
in common hours.

HENRY DAVID THOREAU

DREAM every day.

I believe in the
power of dreams.
I can be anything,
go anywhere.

DES'REE

DREAM every day.

I believe in luck
as much as the
next person—
I'm just not willing
to wait for it.

KOBI YAMADA

DREAM every day.

How many people do you know who spend their lives taxiing down the runway of life, revving their engines, but afraid to take off? We were all designed to fly!

DR. H. PAUL JACOBI

DREAM every day.

Forsake all
inhibitions.
Pursue thy dreams!

WALT WHITMAN

DREAM every day.

Life is short,
so when you
want something,
you really do
have to go for it.

KATE WINSLET

DREAM every day.

Believe it!
High expectations
are the key to
everything.

SAM WALTON

DREAM every day.

Never measure
the height of the
mountain until
you have reached
the top. Then
you will see how
low it was.

DAG HAMMARSKJOLD

DREAM every day.

If you accept
your limitations,
you never go
beyond them.

BRENDAN FRANCIS

DREAM every day.

I don't want to
represent man as
he is, but only
as he might be.

ALBERT CAMUS

People are capable, at any time in their lives, of doing what they dream of.

BETH BINGHAM

DREAM every day.

Never let your
fears hold you
back from pursuing
your hopes.

JOHN F. KENNEDY

DREAM every day.

Throughout the
centuries there
were men who took
first steps down
new roads armed
with nothing but
their own vision.

AYN RAND

DREAM every day.

Fate loves the
fearless.

HOWARD ZENDELL

DREAM every day.

We all grow by
great dreams.
Some let their
great dreams die,
but others nourish
and protect them,
and nurse them
through bad
days until they
bring them to
the sunshine
and the light.

WOODROW WILSON

DREAM every day.

One by one, we
can be the better
world we wish for.

HEIDI WILLS

DREAM every day.

To see one's goal
and to drive
toward it, steeling
one's heart, is
most uplifting.

HENRIK IBSEN

DREAM every day.

Have a go.
Anybody can do it.

ALAN PARKER

DREAM every day.

Per ardua ad astra
(by striving we
reach the stars).

ROYAL AIR FORCE MOTTO

DREAM every day.

The first step
towards getting
somewhere is to
decide that you
are not going
to stay where
you are.

J. PIERPONT MORGAN

DREAM every day.

The guy who
takes a chance,
who walks the
line between the
known and the
unknown, who is
afraid of failure,
will succeed.

GORDON PARKS

DREAM every day.

After the final no
there comes a yes,
and on that yes
the future world
depends.

WALLACE STEVENS

DREAM every day.

We are each
responsible for
our own life—
no other person is
or even can be.

OPRAH WINFREY

DREAM every day.

Why spend your
life making someone
else's dreams?

ORSON WELLS TO ED WOOD

DREAM every day.

I believe that
when you realize
who you really
are, you under-
stand that nothing
can stop you
from becoming
that person.

CHRISTINE LINCOLN

DREAM every day.

It's amazing—you may not realize it, but so much of what you are not is because you are literally standing in your own way of becoming. And what I'm pleading with you about is, get the hell out of your own way!

LEO BUSCAGLIA

DREAM every day.

He who would
learn to fly one
day must first
learn to stand and
walk and run and
climb and dance;
one cannot fly
into flying.

FRIEDRICH NIETZSCHE

DREAM every day.

Life shrinks or
expands in
proportion to
one's courage.

ANAIS NIN

DREAM every day.

They can because
they think they can.

VIRGIL

DREAM every day.

The greatest thing
is to be willing to
give up who we
are in order to
become all that
we can become.

MAX DEPREE

DREAM every day.

The difference
between what
we do, and what
we are capable of
doing, would solve
most of the world's
problems.

MAHATMA GANDHI

DREAM every day.

Nothing splendid
has ever been
achieved except
by those who dared
to believe that
something inside
them was superior
to circumstances.

BRUCE BARTON

DREAM every day.

Between the wish
and the thing life
lies waiting.

UNKNOWN

DREAM every day.

Surround yourself
with people who
believe you can.

DAN ZADRA

DREAM every day.

Keep following
your heart even
when others scoff.

HOWARD SCHULTZ

DREAM every day.

If what's in your
dreams wasn't
already real inside
you, you couldn't
even dream it.

GLORIA STEINEM

DREAM every day.

It is better to
believe than
to disbelieve.
In so doing you
bring everything
to the realm
of possibility.

UNKNOWN

DREAM every day.

Never fear the
space between
your dreams and
reality. If you
can dream it, you
can make it so.

BELVA DAVIS

DREAM every day.

Courage is not the
absence of fear,
but rather the
judgement that
something else is
more important
than fear.

AMBROSE REDMOON

DREAM every day.

Look the world
straight in the eye.

HELEN KELLER

DREAM every day.

The secret to
succeeding is
inner strength.

SHAQUILLE O'NEAL

DREAM every day.

If you don't ask,
you don't get.

MOHANDAS GANDHI

DREAM every day.

Taking chances
helps you grow.

UNKNOWN

DREAM every day.

When you cannot
make up your mind
which of two
evenly balanced
courses of action
you should take—
choose the bolder.

GENERAL W. J. SLIM

Do you seize
opportunities,
or do you let
them slip by?

JOHN GRAY, PH.D.

DREAM every day.

Believe that you
have it, and
you have it.

LATIN PROVERB

DREAM every day.

Act like you
expect to get into
the end zone.

JOE PATERNO

DREAM every day.

Whatever you
want in your life
shall be yours.

BRITNEY SPEARS

DREAM every day.

From small
beginnings come
great things.

PROVERB

DREAM every day.

Rough diamonds
may sometimes be
mistaken for
worthless pebbles.

SIR THOMAS BROWNE

DREAM every day.

We are what
we believe we are.

BENJAMIN N. CARDOZO

DREAM every day.

We've got two lives.
The one we're given
and the one we make.

KOBI YAMADA

DREAM every day.

You have to think
anyway, so why
not think big?

DONALD TRUMP

DREAM every day.

One of these days
is none of these days.

ENGLISH PROVERB

DREAM every day.

Let me tell you
the secret that has
led me to my goal.
My strength lies
solely in my
tenacity.

LOUIS PASTEUR

DREAM every day.

All things come
to those who go
after them.

ROB ESTES

DREAM every day.

Go confidently
in the direction
of your dreams!
Live the life
you've imagined.

HENRY DAVID THOREAU

DREAM every day.

Aim so high you'll
never be bored.

LINDA GIBBONS

DREAM every day.

The barriers are
not erected which
can say to aspiring
talents and
industry, "thus far
and no farther".

LUDWIG VON BEETHOVEN

DREAM every day.

Everyone has in
them something
precious that is
in no one else.

MARTIN BUBER

DREAM every day.

Do you want to
be safe and good,
or do you want to
take a chance
and be great?

JIMMY JOHNSON

DREAM every day.

The future
belongs to those
who believe in
the beauty of their
dreams. In the
long run, we really
do shape our own
lives; and then
together we shape
the world around
us. The process
never ends until
we die.

ELEANOR ROOSEVELT

DREAM every day.

You are the one
who can stretch
your own horizon.

EDGAR MAGNIN

DREAM every day.

Without leaps
of imagination
or dreaming,
we lose the
excitement of
possibilities.
Dreaming, after
all, is a form
of planning.

GLORIA STEINEM

DREAM every day.

One of the greatest
discoveries a man
makes, one of his
great surprises, is
to find he can do
what he was afraid
he couldn't do.

HENRY FORD

DREAM every day.

Most people see
what is, and never
see what can be.

ALBERT EINSTEIN

DREAM every day.

How far is far,
how high is high?
We'll never know
until we try.

FROM SPECIAL OLYMPICS SONG

DREAM every day.

How exciting are
your dreams?
Most people don't
aim too high and
miss, they aim
too low and hit.

BOB MOAWAD

DREAM every day.

I can believe
anything provided
it is incredible.

OSCAR WILDE

DREAM every day.

It's time to start
living the life
you've imagined.

HENRY JAMES

DREAM every day.

Our aspirations
are our
possibilities.

ROBERT BROWNING

DREAM every day.

At least once a
day, allow yourself
the freedom to
think and dream
for yourself.

ALBERT EINSTEIN

DREAM every day.

COMPENDIUM™
PUBLISHING

live inspired.

As you begin to pay attention to your own

stories and what they say about you, you

will enter into the exciting process of becoming,

as you should be, the author of your own

life, the creator of your own possibilities.

MANDY AFTEL

ACKNOWLEDGEMENTS

WITH SPECIAL THANKS TO

Jason Aldrich, Gerry Baird, Jay Baird, Neil Beaton, Doug Cruickshank, Jim Darragh, Jennifer & Matt Ellison, Josie & Rob Estes, Michael Flynn, Jennifer Hurwitz, Liam Lavery, Connie McMartin, Cristal & Brad Olberg, Janet Potter & Family, Aimee Rawlins, Diane Roger, Drew Wilkie, Robert & Mary Anne Wilkie, Heidi & Shale Yamada, Justi, Tote & Caden Yamada, Robert & Val Yamada, Kaz, Kristin, Kyle & Kendyl Yamada, Tai & Joy Yamada, Anne Zadra, August & Arline Zadra and Dan Zadra.

CREDITS

Compiled by Kobi Yamada

Designed by Steve Potter

ISBN: 1-888387-57-2

©2005 Compendium, Incorporated. All rights reserved. No part of this publication may be reproduced or transmitted in any form or by any means, electronic or mechanical, including photocopy, recording, or any storage and retrieval system now known or to be invented without written permission from the publisher. Contact: Compendium, Inc., 6325 212th Street, S.W., Suite K, Lynnwood, WA 98036. Every Day Journals, We Are The Hero of Our Own Story, Compendium, live inspired and the format, design, layout and coloring used in this book are trademarks and/or trade dress of Compendium, Incorporated. This book may be ordered directly from the publisher, but please try your local bookstore first. Call us at 800-91-IDEAS or come see our full line of inspiring products at www.compendiuminc.com

Printed in China